Ursula Reikes

Dedication

To my mother and father, Edward and Luise Golisz, for always believing in me, and for teaching me the value of hard work to fulfill my dreams; and to my husband, John, for his love, encouragement, and support, and for all those wonderful dinners.

Acknowledgments

My sincerest thanks to the following people for their contribution to my passion.

Bev Schmidt—for teaching the first quilting class I took fourteen years ago;

Deborah Aracic—for fourteen years of friendship that has grown beyond our passion for quilting;

Trish Carey—for her wonderful ideas, encouragement, and friendship;

Barbara Weiland and That Patchwork Place—for giving me the job of a lifetime;

And my special friends throughout the years who have encouraged my pedestrian creativity.

And, a special thank you to Hoffman of California Fabrics and Alexander Henry Fabrics for permission to adapt graphic designs from their fabrics to embellish the pages of this book.

Credits

Editor-in-Chief . . . . Barbara Weiland
Managing Editor . . . . Greg Sharp
Copy Editor . . . . Liz McGehee
Proofreader . . . . Tina Cook
Text and Cover Design . . . . Kay Green
Typesetting . . . . Julianna Reynolds
Photography . . . . Brent Kane
Illustration and Graphics . . . . Laurel Strand

Quilts for Baby: Easy as A, B, C ©
©1993 by Ursula Golisz Reikes

Martingale & Company
19021 120th Ave. NE, Suite 102
Bothell, WA 98011-9511 USA
www.martingale-pub.com

Printed in China
15 14 13 12 11   31 30 29 28 27

Reikes, Ursula Golisz
    Quilts for baby : easy as ABC / Ursula Golisz Reikes
      p. cm.
    ISBN 978-1-56477-041-7
    1. Quilting—Patterns. 2. Patchwork—Patterns
    3. Crib quilts.
  I. Title.
TT835.R44   1993
746.9'7—dc20

                          93-28647
                              CIP

Quilts for Baby: Easy as A, B, C

Introduction 4

General Directions 5

   Supplies 5

   Selecting Fabrics 5

   Preparing Fabrics 6

   Cutting .6

   Piecing .8

   Pressing 9

   Assembling the Quilt Top 9

   Adding Borders 10

   Backing 11

   Making a Quilt Sandwich 11

   Quilting 12

   Binding 13

   Labeling Your Quilt 15

Anatomy of a Quilt 16

Quilts for Baby 18

   One Patch 18

   Framed One Patch 20

   Four Patch 30

   Rail Fence 32

   Log Cabin 34

   Log Cabin Zoo 36

   Courthouse Steps 38

   Hourglass 40

   Friendship Star 42

   Shoo Fly 44

   Easy Attic Windows 46

Gallery 21

Introduction

I make quilts for babies, not for their parents, and not necessarily to match the decor of their rooms. I make quilts to be used (although some parents insist on putting them on the walls). I want them to be dragged around the house, into the car, and into the yard. If they are bright and busy, they will be noticed, used, and loved.

Many of us have fantasies about making a one-of-a-kind heirloom quilt for a favorite child, but busy schedules and life in general have a habit of getting in the way and taking up precious stitching time. Some of us just want to make a little something special for a special little one. I wrote this book to show you that you don't have to invest a lot of time or money to make any one of the simple baby quilts in this book. As a bonus, these quilts are great projects for beginners because the blocks are so simple. I've used speedy rotary cutting and easy strip-piecing methods to make them even easier. Most of the quilt tops can be pieced in three to five hours, depending upon your skill level. Finishing time depends on whether you choose to hand or machine quilt. Anyone can easily make one of these baby quilts in a few evenings, or in a weekend.

The patterns are timeless and have been favorites of quilters for many generations.

For a majority of the featured quilts, you make six blocks, then add two borders—and that's it! The top is finished and you are ready to quilt! Some quilts have nine blocks and one has thirty-six, but even the thirty-six-block quilt is a snap to make. If you are a new quilter and unfamiliar with the piece that make up a quilt, be sure to refer to "Anatomy of a Quilt" on pages 16–17.

In addition to providing simple patterns, I've created the quilts in this book to illustrate how fabrics can be combined into exciting, colorful quilts—quilts that have movement, which invites young eyes to wander around the surface and explore the design shapes. The possibilities for combining these playful fabrics are endless.

Each year, the 100% cotton "kids'" prints get better—more colorful and more playful—and are available in patterns that follow the latest fads. Dinosaurs have been big for several years now, but who knows what will be hot next year? The size and simplicity of the quilt blocks in this book make them a perfect showcase for your favorite juvenile prints from year to year.

I invite you to let the child within you come out and play. Experiment, be daring, be bold—but most of all, have fun. And remember, you are making these quilts for the babies, not for their parents.

For more quick-and-easy quilts, look for *More Quilts for Baby: Easy as ABC,* and *Even More Quilts for Baby: Easy as ABC* by Ursula Reikes.

General Directions

As with any quilting project, you will need a few basic supplies to make the quilts in this book.

Supplies

100% cotton fabric

100% cotton thread

Sewing machine in good working order, with a walking foot or a darning foot for machine quilting

Rotary-cutting equipment, including the following:

rotary cutter

cutting mat

6" x 24" ruler for cutting strips

12" x 12" square ruler for squaring up blocks

Fine, thin pins

Scissors

Seam ripper

Iron and ironing board

Marking pencil

Safety pins

Selecting Fabrics

When selecting fabrics for a baby quilt, my motto is "the bigger the print, the brighter the colors, the better!" I want the babies who receive my quilts to notice the colors and patterns. I prefer to use 100% cotton because it is easy to handle and basically baby-proof since it launders so well. My personal favorites are the bright, bold prints made by Hoffman California Fabrics and Alexander Henry Fabrics. These two fabric companies have been producing great kids' prints for many years.

I like to combine several different prints in one quilt. When deciding which prints and colors to put together, I use the following guidelines:

- Combine pure colors (primary colors) with other pure colors.
- Combine tints (soft pastels) with other tints.
- Vary the scale or busyness of the prints. Too much of the same scale can be boring.

The key is variety. *Don't be afraid to mix prints.* While a large-scale print may seem overwhelming in a whole piece, it takes on a whole new appearance when cut into a 2"-wide strip. Cutting up a large-scale print creates a lot of movement in a quilt top. Combining several large-scale prints creates a quilt that forces the eyes to move around the quilt and explore all the shapes.

I'm always on the lookout for unusual prints. See "Mickey in the Attic" on page 27. I cut up boxer shorts for the center of the blocks in this quilt. While thumbing through a mail-order catalog, I spotted the Mickey Mouse™ boxer shorts, so I ordered several in the Extra-Large size. After washing the shorts to remove the sizing and undoing all the seams, I carefully planned how to cut them up so I could get the maximum number of 6½" squares possible from each pair. By planning the cutting carefully, I was able to get the nine Mickeys you see in the quilt from one pair of boxer shorts.

If the design in the fabric is too large to fit comfortably inside a 6" window, make the "window" square larger and then adjust the other components in the quilt accordingly. If the design is too small, add a frame around the design to make a larger square.

Of course, you can do the same thing when cutting fabric yardage in order to center specific design motifs within a particular piece. The quilt "Animal Crackers" on page 21 is another example of selectively cutting a "theme" or story fabric to showcase in a block.

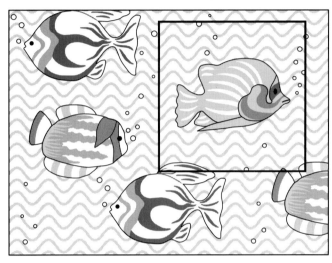

Cutting specific designs from fabric requires extra yardage. Plan your cuts carefully.

Preparing Fabrics

I prewash all fabrics in warm water, without detergent, then tumble dry and iron them before putting them away. This way, there's never any confusion about whether or not a piece in my fabric closet has been prewashed. When I'm working on a project at 3 a.m., the last thing I want to do is start the washer and wake up the entire household!

All yardage requirements for the quilts in this book are based on 42" of usable width after prewashing. If your fabric is narrower than 42", you may need additional yardage so you can cut another strip.

Cutting

Instructions are for rotary cutting all pieces, and all measurements include standard ¼"-wide seam allowances. For those unfamiliar with rotary cutting, a brief introduction is provided below. For more detailed information on the subject, see Donna Thomas' *Shortcuts: A Concise Guide to Rotary Cutting.*

1. Fold the fabric and match selvages, aligning the crosswise and lengthwise grains as much as possible. Place the folded edge closest to you on the cutting mat. To make a cut at a right angle to the fold, align a square ruler along the folded edge of the fabric. Then place a long, straight ruler to the left of the square ruler, just covering the uneven raw edges of the left side of the fabric.

   Remove the square ruler and cut along the right edge of the ruler, rolling the rotary cutter away from you. Discard this strip. (Reverse this procedure if you are left-handed.)

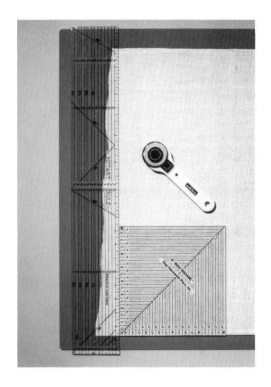

2. To cut strips, align the required measurement on the ruler with the newly cut edge of the fabric. For example, to cut a 3"-wide strip, place the 3" mark on the ruler on the edge of the fabric. All of the measurements for cut strips include ¼"-wide seam allowances. Therefore, a 3"-wide strip, with a ¼"-wide seam allowance on each long edge (for a total of ½"), will finish to 2½" wide.

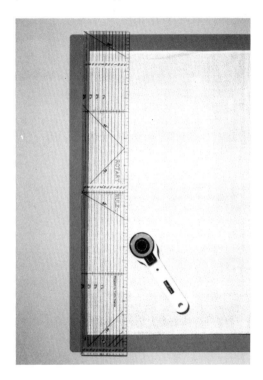

3. To cut squares, cut strips in the required widths. Trim away the selvage ends of the strip. Align the required measurement on the ruler with the left edge of the strip and cut a square. Continue cutting until you have the number of squares needed.

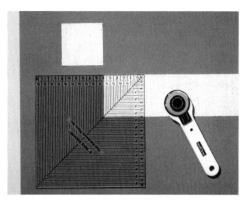

4. For some quilts, you will cut strips and then sew them together in strip sets. Then you will cut squares from the strip sets. First, trim the short end to square it up. Then align the required measurement on the ruler with the left edge of the strip set and cut the required number of squares.

Safety Tip

Always keep the safety cover of the rotary cutter closed when not in use.

Piecing

The blocks in this book are simple to make. Even sewing the triangles together is easy. The most important thing to remember is to *maintain a consistent ¼"-wide seam allowance throughout your piecing.* Otherwise, the quilt block will not be the desired finished size. If that happens, the size of everything else in the quilt is affected—alternate blocks, sashing, and borders. Measurements for all components of the quilt are based on blocks that finish to the desired size plus ¼" on each edge for the seam allowances.

Establishing an Accurate Seam Guide

Take the time now to establish an exact ¼"-wide seam guide on your machine. Some machines have a special quilting foot designed so that the right-hand and left-hand edges of the foot measure exactly ¼" from the center needle position. This feature allows you to use the edge of the presser foot to guide the edge of the fabric for a perfect ¼"-wide seam allowance.

If your machine doesn't have such a foot, you can create a seam guide so it will be easy to stitch an accurate ¼"-wide seam allowance.

1. Place a ruler or piece of graph paper with four squares to the inch under your presser foot.
2. Gently lower the needle onto the first ¼" line from the right edge of the ruler or paper. Place several layers of tape, a piece of moleskin (available in drugstores), or a magnetic seam guide along the right-hand edge of the ruler or paper, so that it does not interfere with the feed dog. Test your new guide to make sure your seams are ¼" wide; if not, readjust your guide.

Safety Tip

Strong magnets can damage computerized sewing machines, especially older models. If your machine is computerized, remove the magnetic seam guide when you finish sewing and store it away from the machine.

When your blocks are complete, take the time to square them up. Use a square ruler to measure your blocks and make sure they are the desired finished size plus an extra ¼" on each edge for seam allowances. For example, if you are making 6" blocks, they should all measure 6½" before you sew them together. If the size of the blocks varies greatly, trim the larger ones to match the size of the smallest one. Be sure to trim all four sides; otherwise your block will be lopsided. If your blocks are not the finished size given in the quilt plan you are following, you will have to adjust all the other components accordingly.

Piecing Half-Square Triangle Units

Three of the quilts in this book, "Shoo Fly" (page 44), "Friendship Star (page 42), and "Easy Attic Windows" (page 46) require half-square triangle units.

1. Cut squares the size given in the quilt directions. Draw a diagonal line from corner to corner on the back of the lightest fabric.

2. Place the square with the drawn line on top of another square, right sides together. Sew ¼" away from the drawn line on both sides.

3. Cut on the drawn line. Every pair of squares you sew together yields 2 half-square triangle units.

Tip

Take the time to pin while piecing. I have learned from experience that pinning is extremely helpful in aligning pieces and matching corners and points.

Pressing

Pressing is important and helps the pieces fit together correctly. I use a steam iron and set it on "Cotton."

1. Press the stitches flat along the seam line after sewing. This relaxes the thread and smooths out any puckers.
2. Working from the right side, press the seam toward the darker fabric. Be careful not to stretch the pieces out of shape as you press.

Assembling the Quilt Top

When you have made all the blocks and have cut the sashing, if necessary, it's time to put all the pieces together to make the quilt top.

1. Arrange the blocks as shown in the quilt plan provided with each quilt.
2. Sew the blocks together in horizontal rows; press the seams in opposite directions from row to row so the seams of the blocks will butt up against each other when you join the rows.

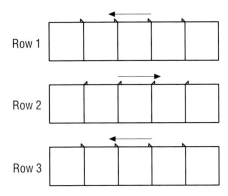

3. Sew the rows together, making sure to match the seams between the blocks.

For quilts with sashing strips and cornerstones, arrange blocks, sashing strips, and cornerstones as shown in the quilt plan. Sew the blocks and sashing strips together in horizontal rows; press seams toward the sashing strips. Sew the sashing strips and cornerstones together in horizontal rows; press the seams toward the sashing strips. Sew the rows together, making sure to match the seams.

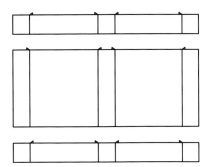

Adding Borders

For best results, do not cut border strips and sew them directly to the quilt sides without measuring first. This method often results in a quilt with wavy borders. The edges of a quilt often measure slightly longer than the distance through the quilt center due to stretching during construction. Sometimes, each edge is a different length. Measure the quilt top through the center in both directions to determine how long to cut the border strips. This step ensures that the finished quilt will be as straight and as "square" as possible, without wavy edges.

Measurements for cutting borders are provided with each quilt and are based on blocks sewn with accurate ¼"-wide seam allowances. To be safe, measure your completed blocks to be sure they are the correct size before cutting border strips. Remember, your blocks should be ½" larger than the finished size on all sides.

If your completed blocks are a different size than required, or you added more blocks to increase the size of the quilt, then you will need to measure the quilt top to determine the correct border lengths.

1. Measure the length of the quilt top through the center. Cut border strips to that measurement (piecing as necessary); mark the centers of the quilt top and the border strips. Pin the borders to the sides of the quilt top, matching the center marks and ends and easing as necessary. Sew the border strips in place. Press the seams toward the border.

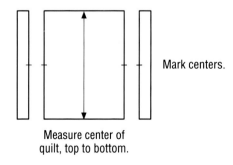

Measure center of quilt, top to bottom.

2. Measure the width of the quilt through the center, including the side borders just added. Cut border strips to that measurement (piecing as necessary); mark the center of the quilt top and the border strips. Pin the border strips to the top and bottom edges of the quilt top, matching the center marks and ends and easing as necessary. Sew the border strips in place. Press the seams toward the border.

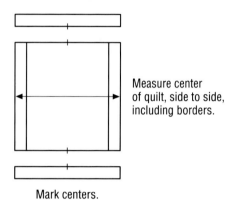

Measure center of quilt, side to side, including borders.

Mark centers.

Borders with Corner Squares

1. Measure the width and length of the quilt through the center. Cut border strips to that measurement. Mark the centers of the quilt edges and the border strips. Pin the side borders to opposite sides of the quilt, matching centers and ends and easing as necessary. Sew the side border strips, and press the seams toward the border.

2. Cut corner squares of the required size. Sew one corner square to each end of the remaining border strips; press seams toward the border strip. Pin the border strips to the top and bottom edges of the quilt. Match centers, seams between the border strip and corner square, and ends, easing as necessary. Sew the border strips in place. Press the seams toward the border.

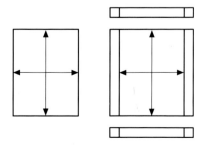

Changing the Quilt Size

Most of the quilts in this book consist of only six or nine large blocks. With just a little more yardage and a little more time, you can easily enlarge any of them. Simply add another row of blocks or another border, or increase the size of the borders. Just remember to adjust the measurements of the other components in the quilt to fit the larger quilt top.

Backing

Always cut the backing larger than the quilt top. This extra allows for slight shifting of the layers that may occur while you quilt and for the shrinkage that often occurs when layers are quilted. Yardage requirements for backings are based on cutting the backing a total of 4" larger than the quilt top all the way around. For example, cut a 46" x 46" backing for a quilt top that measures 42" x 42". Since the standard width for cotton fabric is 42"–44", one length of fabric is not enough for a backing of this size. The preferred method to piece the backing is to cut one length in half and sew to each side of a second length as shown. Cut excess fabric and save the leftovers for other projects.

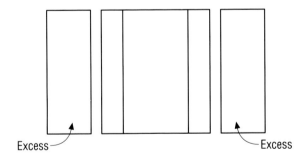

Excess · Excess

Backing Options

There are a couple of different ways I use what I have on hand to make the backing the desired size.

1. I often piece the backs from a variety of fabrics to use up leftover fabric. There's no reason the back can't be as much fun as the front. Determine the required backing size and cut leftover

fabric into strips or squares. Then sew them together randomly or in an interesting pattern, until you have achieved the required size.

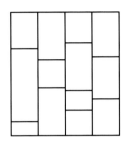

2. If a piece of backing is only 3" or 4" shorter than what I need, I cut strips from leftover fabric used on the front of the quilt; then I add a strip of fabric to one or more sides, or diagonally across the center, to make a backing of the required size.

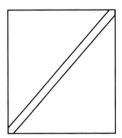

Making a Quilt Sandwich

The quilt sandwich is made up of the quilt top, batting, and backing. A thin, low-loft batting works well for either hand or machine quilting. Unroll the batting and let it relax overnight before you layer your quilt. Cut the backing and batting a total of 4" larger than the quilt top, all the way around.

1. Place backing, wrong side up, on a large table. Use masking tape or large binder clamps to anchor the backing to the table, making sure it's flat and wrinkle-free. Be careful not to stretch the backing out of shape.

2. Place the batting on top of the backing, smoothing out all wrinkles.
3. Place the pressed quilt top on top of the batting. Smooth out any wrinkles and make sure the edges of the quilt top are parallel to the edges of the backing.
4. Baste with safety pins (or needle and thread, if you prefer) to keep the layers together. Place pins about 6"–8" apart, away from the area you intend to quilt. Sewing-machine needles and safety pins do not get along!

Quilt top
Batting
Pins
Backing
Masking tape

Quilting

All of my quilts are machine quilted because I want the babies for whom they are made to receive their quilts before they get their drivers' licenses. I love the look of hand quilting and admire anyone who has the patience and time to do it, but I don't have that kind of time.

The quilts in this book are machine quilted with a combination of straight-line and free-motion quilting. I use cotton or rayon thread for machine quilting. Finding a thread to blend with all the colors and prints can be difficult, but red seems to work with most of the primary-colored quilts. I recently tried some variegated threads, which worked particularly well for multicolored quilt tops.

1. For straight-line quilting, it is extremely helpful to have a walking foot to help the quilt layers feed through the machine without shifting or puckering. Some machines have a built-in walking foot; other machines require a separate attachment. Use straight-line quilting to create allover grids, diagonal straight lines, and to outline quilt and "quilt in the ditch."

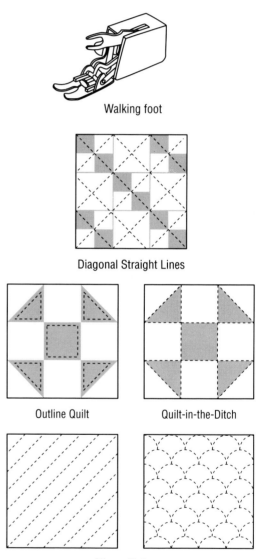

Walking foot

Diagonal Straight Lines

Outline Quilt   Quilt-in-the-Ditch

Allover Patterns

2. For free-motion quilting, you need a darning foot and the ability to drop the feed dog on the machine. With free-

motion quilting, you do not turn the fabric under the needle but instead guide the fabric in the direction of the design. Use free-motion quilting to outline quilt a pattern in the fabric or to create scribbles, stippling, and many other curved designs.

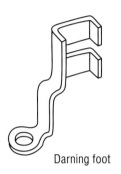

Darning foot

Large Stippling

Scribbles

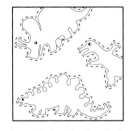

Free-Motion Outline Quilt

To learn more about quilting by machine or by hand, refer to one of the many fine books available on the subject.

Binding

I prefer double-fold, straight-cut binding. I use double-fold bias binding when I want to change the direction of a print for the binding, such as placing a stripe on the diagonal around the outer finished edge.

See the "Dinosaur Frolic" quilt (page 28) or the "Alphabet Soup" quilt (page 25) for examples.

To cut double, straight-grain binding strips:
Cut the required number of 2½"-wide strips. Cut across the width of the fabric. You will need enough strips to go around the perimeter of the quilt plus 4" or 5" for seams and the corners in a mitered fold.

To cut double-fold bias binding strips:
1. Fold a square of fabric on the diagonal.

Bias fold

OR

Fold a ½-yard piece as shown in the diagrams below, paying careful attention to the location of the lettered corners.

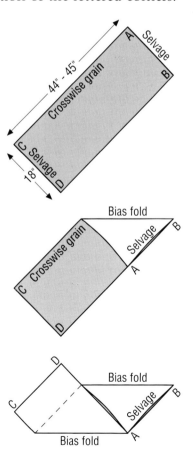

2. Cut strips 2½" wide, cutting perpendicular to the folds as shown.

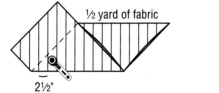

To attach binding:

1. Sew strips, right sides together, to make one long piece of binding. Press seams open.

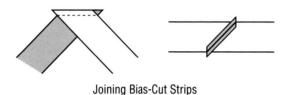

Joining Bias-Cut Strips

If you cut the strips on the straight grain, join strips at right angles and stitch across the corner as shown. Trim excess fabric.

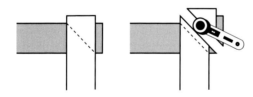

Joining Straight-Cut Strips

2. Fold the strip in half lengthwise, wrong sides together, and press.

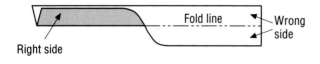

3. Turn under ¼" at a 45° angle at one end of the strip and press. Turning it

under at an angle distributes the bulk so you won't have a lump where the two ends of the binding meet.

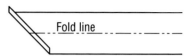

4. Starting on one side of the quilt, stitch the binding to the quilt, keeping the raw edges even with the quilt top edge; use a ¼"-wide seam. End the stitching ¼" from the corner of the quilt and backstitch. Clip the thread.

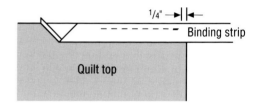

5. Turn the quilt so that you will be stitching down the next side. Fold the binding up, away from the quilt.

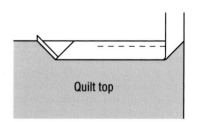

6. Fold binding back down onto itself, parallel with the edge of the quilt top. Begin stitching at the edge, backstitching to secure.

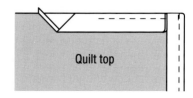

7. Repeat on the remaining edges and corners of the quilt. When you reach the beginning of the binding, overlap the beginning stitches by about 1" and cut away any excess binding, trimming the end at a 45° angle. Tuck the end of the binding into the fold and finish the seam.

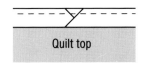

8. Trim away excess batting and backing. Fold the binding over the raw edges of the quilt to the back and blindstitch in place with the folded edge covering the row of machine stitching. A miter will form at each corner. Blindstitch the mitered corners in place.

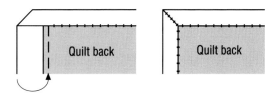

Labeling Your Quilt

Don't forget to make a label for your quilt that includes your name, city and state, the date, and to whom the quilt was given, if it is a gift. Machine embroider (if your machine has that capability) or write the information on a piece of muslin with a permanent marking pen and sew the label to the back of the finished quilt.

Anatomy of a Quilt

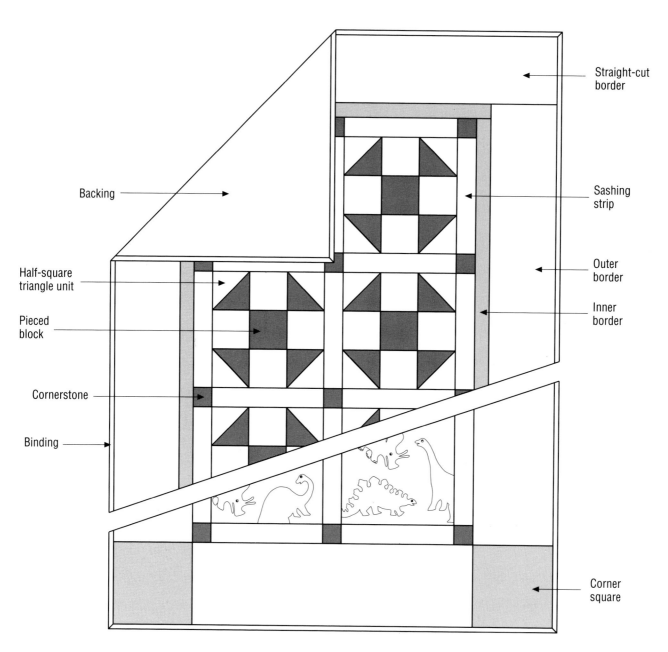

These are the pieces that make up a quilt top.

Backing

A lage piece of fabric that covers the back of a quilt. It may be pieced from more than one piece of fabric for a larger quilt.

Batting

A layer inside the quilt, sandwiched between the quilt top and the quilt backing.

Binding

A strip of fabric, cut on either the straight of grain or the bias, sewn to and wrapped around the edges of the quilt to finish the quilt.

Borders

The area surrounding the main body of the quilt top that acts like a frame on a picture. One or more fabric strips of varying widths may be added.

Straight-Cut Borders

A border that is applied in two steps. Border strips are sewn to opposite sides first, then to the top and bottom of the quilt top.

Borders with Corner Squares

A border that is applied in three steps. Border strips are sewn to opposite sides first. Then, corner squares are sewn to each end of the remaining top and bottom border strips. Finally, the border strips plus corner squares are attached to the top and bottom of the quilt top.

Corner Square

A square of fabric used to join adjacent border strips.

Cornerstone

A square of fabric used to join two sashing strips where they intersect.

Half-Square Triangle Unit

A square made up of two right-angle triangles. This is a common unit in many patchwork quilts.

Quilt Top

The upper layer of a quilt that is pieced to form the overall design.

Pieced Block

Small pieces of fabric in various shapes sewn together to form a larger design.

Sashing Strips

A strip of fabric sewn between the blocks and between rows of blocks.

One Patch

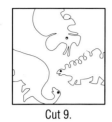

Cut 9.

Color Photo: Dinosaur Frolic on page 28
Quilt Size: 39½" x 39½"
Finished Block Size: 7"

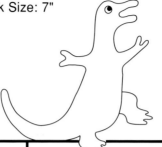

Materials *44"-wide fabric*		Cutting *Cut all strips across the fabric width.*		
		First Cut		Second Cut
	Yardage	*No. of Strips*	*Strip Size*	*Dimensions*
Center squares	½ yd.*	2	7½" x 42"	9 ▢ – 7½" x 7½"
Cornerstones	⅛ yd.	1	2½" x 42"	16 ▢ – 2½" x 2½"
Sashing	½ yd.	5	2½" x 42"	24 ▭ – 2½" x 7½"
Border	⅞ yd.	4	5½" x 29½"	
Corner squares	¼ yd.	1	5½" x 42"	4 ▢ – 5½" x 5½"
Binding	⅜ yd.**	4	2½" x 42"	
Backing	1¼ yds.			

*You will need additional yardage if you want to center specific design motifs within each square.
**Use ½ yd. for bias binding.

Quilt Top Assembly

1. Arrange squares, sashing strips, and cornerstones as shown below.

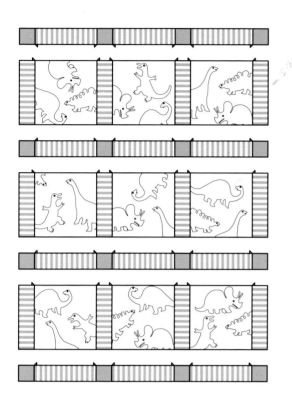

2. Sew cornerstones and sashing strips together in horizontal rows. Press seams toward the sashing strips.
3. Sew sashing strips and blocks together in horizontal rows. Press seams toward the sashing strips.
4. Sew rows together, making sure to match the seams between each block.

Quilt Finishing

1. Sew border strips to opposite sides of the quilt top. Sew 5½" x 5½" corner squares to each end of top and bottom border strips. Attach to the top and bottom edges of quilt top. See page 10.

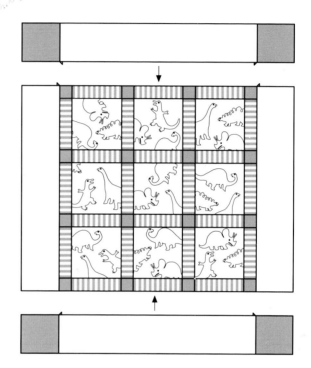

2. Layer the quilt top with batting and backing; baste. Quilt as desired.
3. Bind the edges of the quilt. See pages 13–15.

Note: If you use a striped fabric for the binding as I did, cut the binding strips on the bias so the stripes are on the diagonal around the outer edge of the completed quilt.

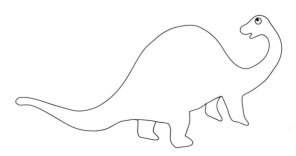

Framed One Patch

Color Photo: Sweet Teddy Bears on page 22
Quilt Size: 34½" x 44½"
Finished Block Size: 8"

Make 6.

Materials *44"-wide fabric*		Cutting *Cut all strips across the fabric width.*			
		First Cut		**Second Cut**	
	Yardage	*No. of Strips*	*Strip Size*	*Dimensions*	
Center squares	¼ yd.*	1	7" x 42"	6	– 7" x 7"
Frames	¼ yd.	5	1¼" x 42"	12	– 1¼" x 7"
				12	– 1¼" x 8½"
Cornerstones	⅛ yd.	1	2½" x 42"	12	– 2½" x 2½"
Sashing	½ yd.	5	2½" x 42"	17	– 2½" x 8½"
Border (sides)	⅞ yd.	2	6½" x 32½"		
(top/bottom)		2	6½" x 34½"		
Binding	⅜ yd.	4	2½" x 42"		
Backing	1⅜ yds.				

*You will need additional yardage if you want to center specific design motifs within each square.

Quilt Top Assembly

1. Sew 1¼" x 7" framing strips to opposite sides of each 7" x 7" square. Sew 1¼" x 8½" framing strips to the top and bottom edges of each square.

(continued on page 29)

GALLERY

Animal Crackers, by Ursula Reikes, 1993, 38½" x 50½". An oversized central block in this easy Log Cabin variation is the perfect place to spotlight favorite zoo animals. Made for Kelly Hailstone, Issaquah, Washington. I chose this jungle print for Kelly because his parents, Robin and Oscar, love animals as much I do and have their own zoo at home.

Sweet Teddy Bears, by Ursula Reikes, 1993, 34½" x 44½". I had to make this quilt to show everyone that I *could* make something soft and sweet! Use a special print for the block, then add simple sashing and cornerstones. What could be easier?

Jelly Bean Jungle, by Ursula Reikes, 1993, 42" x 42". Busy prints in bright colors disguise the simple Courthouse Steps block in this happy, colorful quilt.

Circus Stars, by Ursula Reikes, 1993, 38½" x 38½". Simple Four Patch blocks are set off with alternating blocks cut from a circus print that was also used for the wide outer border. This is my idea of "soft" for those who don't want to use primary colors. Choose a medium-scale conversational print first, then a coordinating print and a solid. Made for Marie Elena Larsen, Redmond, Washington.

Confetti Sparkler, by Ursula Reikes, 1993, 38¼" x 46½". Strip-pieced triangles in crayon brights sparkle against a confetti background in this appealing quilt. This one is up for grabs!

A Star is Born! by Ursula Reikes, 1993, 36½" x 47½". Scrappy stars made from other quilt leftovers twirl and whirl across this quilt. Use a different print for each one and frame them with bright sashing and a bold border. Made for "Baby" Kane. Daddy Brent is our great photographer at That Patchwork Place.

Blast Off! by Ursula Reikes, 1993, 38½" x 44½". Colorful rocket ships surround a riot of bright primary colors in this easy Rail Fence design. Made for Robert Leighton Potter, Pleasanton, California.

Alphabet Soup, by Ursula Reikes, 1993, 38½" x 44½". This quilt is a brighter version of the Rail Fence block. Colorful alphabet fabric and bright, printed stripes are defined by a lighter print in the rails. Made for Dominic Patrick Sena, Half Moon Bay, California.

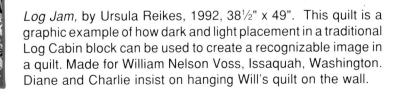

Log Jam, by Ursula Reikes, 1992, 38½" x 49". This quilt is a graphic example of how dark and light placement in a traditional Log Cabin block can be used to create a recognizable image in a quilt. Made for William Nelson Voss, Issaquah, Washington. Diane and Charlie insist on hanging Will's quilt on the wall.

Something's Fishy in the Attic by Ursula Reikes, 1993, 38½" x 38½". Easy-to-piece Attic Windows surround colorful fish in this quilt. It uses the same center blocks as shown below, but has a light blue version of the border fabric.

Something's Fishy in the Attic, by Ursula Reikes, 1993, 38½" x 38½". This quilt was made for Danielle Marie Golden, Key Largo, Florida. Danielle's father, Neal, was my scuba-diving instructor. I'm sure it won't be long before she's introduced to the beautiful world beneath the waves.

Mickey in the Attic, by Ursula Reikes, 1993, 38½" x 38½". What better way to use a pair of boxer shorts! This one's for me.

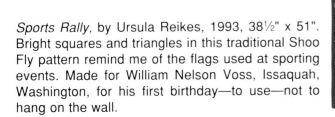

Sports Rally, by Ursula Reikes, 1993, 38½" x 51". Bright squares and triangles in this traditional Shoo Fly pattern remind me of the flags used at sporting events. Made for William Nelson Voss, Issaquah, Washington, for his first birthday—to use—not to hang on the wall.

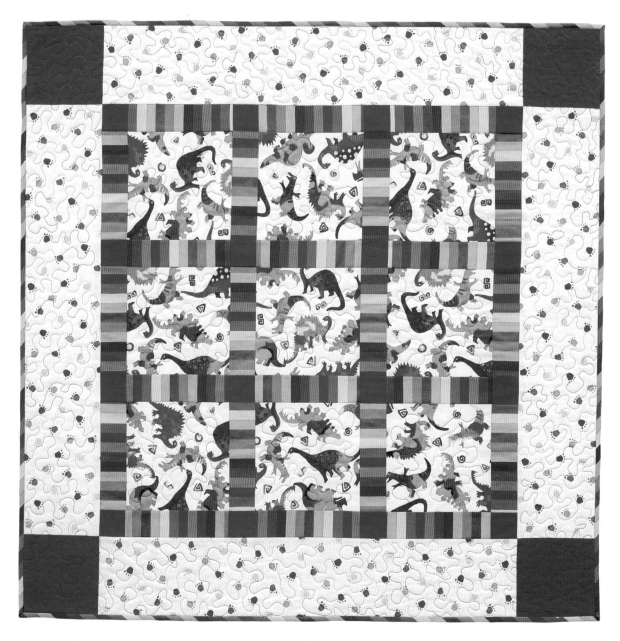

Dinosaur Frolic, by Ursula Reikes, 1993, 39½" x 39½". Even though the one-patch design, surrounded by striped sashing, is a very simple pattern, a colorful print and a bold stripe add lots of color and movement to the finished quilt.

(continued from page 20)

2. Arrange squares, sashing strips, and cornerstones as shown.

3. Sew cornerstones and sashing strips together in horizontal rows. Press seams toward sashing strips.
4. Sew sashing strips and blocks together in horizontal rows. Press seams toward sashing strips.
5. Sew rows together, making sure to match the seams between the blocks.

Quilt Finishing

1. Sew border strips to the long sides first, then to the top and bottom edges of the quilt top. See page 10.
2. Layer the quilt top with batting and backing; baste. Quilt as desired.
3. Bind the edges of the quilt. See pages 13–15.

Four Patch

Make 18.

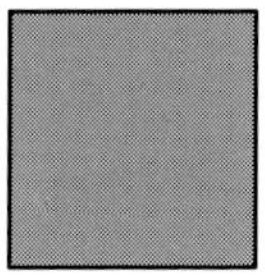

Cut 18.

Color Photo: Circus Stars on page 23
Quilt Size: 38½" x 38½"
Finished Block Size: 4"

Materials *44"-wide fabric*		Cutting *Cut all strips across the fabric width.*	
	Yardage	*No. of Strips*	*Strip Size*
Fabric A	¼ yd.	3	2½" x 42"
Fabric B	¼ yd.	3	2½" x 42"
Fabric C	⅜ yd.	2	4½" x 42"*
Inner border (sides)	⅜ yd.	2	2½" x 24½"
(top/bottom)		2	2½" x 28½"
Outer border (sides)	⅞ yd.	2	5½" x 28½"
(top/bottom)		2	5½" x 38½"
Binding	⅜ yd.	4	2½" x 42"
Backing	1¼ yds.		

*See step 3 on page 31 for additional cutting directions.

Quilt Top Assembly

1. Make 3 strip sets as shown below. Press all seams toward the darker fabric. Crosscut strip sets into 36 segments, each 2½" wide.

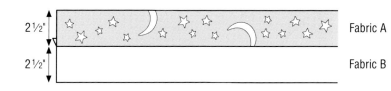

2½"   Fabric A

2½"   Fabric B

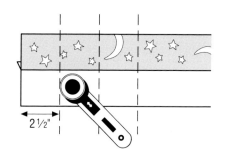

Fabric A

Fabric B

2½"

2. Make 18 Four Patch blocks as shown below.

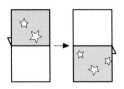

Make 18.

3. From the 4½"-wide strips of Fabric C, cut 18 squares, each 4½" x 4½".

4. Arrange Four Patch blocks and 4½" squares of Fabric C as shown below. Sew blocks together in horizontal rows. Press seams in opposite directions from row to row.

5. Sew rows together, making sure to match the seams between the blocks.

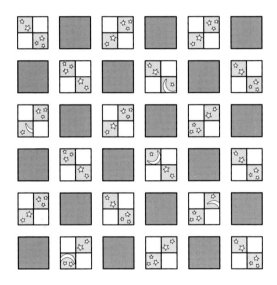

Quilt Finishing

1. Sew the inner border to sides first, then to the top and bottom edges of the quilt top. Repeat for outer border. See page 10.
2. Layer the quilt top with batting and backing; baste. Quilt as desired.
3. Bind the edges of the quilt. See pages 13–15.

Rail Fence

Make 20.

Color Photo: Blast Off! on page 24
and Alphabet Soup on page 25
Quilt Size: 38½" x 44½"
Finished Block Size: 6"

Materials 44"-wide fabric		Cutting Cut all strips across the fabric width.	
	Yardage	*No. of Strips*	*Strip Size*
Fabric A	⅜ yd.	4	2½" x 42"
Fabric B	⅜ yd.	4	2½" x 42"
Fabric C	⅜ yd.	4	2½" x 42"
Inner border (sides)	¼ yd.	2	1½" x 30½"
(top/bottom)		2	1½" x 26½"
Outer border (sides)	1 yd.	2	6½" x 32½"
(top/bottom)		2	6½" x 38½"
Binding	½ yd.	5	2½" x 42"
Backing	1⅜ yds.		

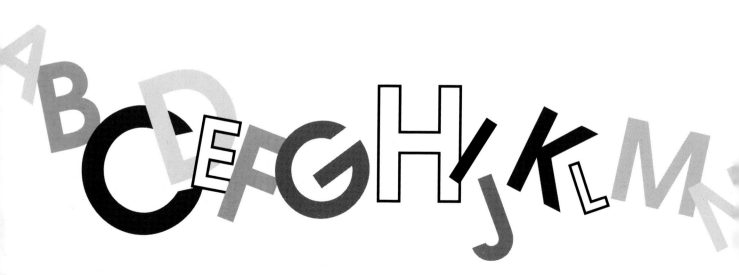

Quilt Top Assembly

1. Make 4 strip sets as shown. Press all seams toward the darker fabrics.

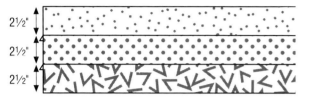

2. Crosscut the strip sets into 20 squares, each 6½" x 6½"*.

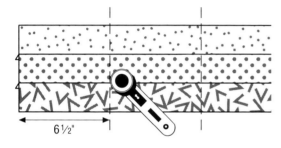

   *Measure the width of the strip set before cutting. If it is not 6½" wide, then crosscut your strip sets into squares using the width of your strip set. For example, if the strip set is only 6" wide, then crosscut the strip set into 6" squares. The end result must be a **square** Rail Fence block.*

3. Arrange the blocks as shown. Sew the blocks together in horizontal rows. Press the seams in opposite directions from row to row.

4. Sew rows together, making sure to match the seams between the blocks.

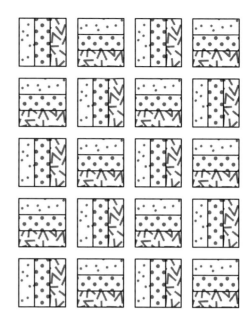

Quilt Finishing

1. Sew the inner border to the sides first, then to the top and bottom edges of the quilt top. Repeat with the outer border strips. See page 10.
2. Layer the quilt top with batting and backing; baste. Quilt as desired.
3. Bind the edges of the quilt. See pages 13–15.

Note: If you use a striped fabric for the binding as I did in Alphabet Soup, cut the binding strips on the bias so the stripes are on the diagonal around the outer edge of the completed quilt.

Log Cabin

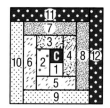

Make 6.

Color Photo: Log Jam on page 25
Quilt Size: 38½" x 49"
Finished Block Size: 10½"

Materials
44"-wide fabric

Cutting
Cut all strips across the fabric width.

	Yardage	No. of Strips	Strip Size
Center	⅛ yd.	1	2" x 15"
Light 1	¼ yd.	1	2" x 15" for Log 1
		1	2" x 42" for Log 2
Light 2	¼ yd.	2	2" x 42" for Logs 5 and 6
Light 3	¼ yd.	3	2" x 42" for Logs 9 and 10
Dark 1	¼ yd.	2	2" x 42" for Logs 3 and 4
Dark 2	¼ yd.	3	2" x 42" for Logs 7 and 8
Dark 3	⅜ yd.	4	2" x 42" for Logs 11 and 12
Inner border (sides)	½ yd.	2	3½" x 32"
(top/bottom)		2	3½" x 27½"
Outer border (sides)	1 yd.	2	6" x 38"
(top/bottom)		2	6" x 38½"
Binding	½ yd.	5	2½" x 42"
Backing	1½ yds.		

Quilt Top Assembly

1. To quick piece the 2 squares in the center of the block, sew 1 strip set as shown below. Press the seam away from the center fabric. Crosscut the strip set into 6 segments, each 2" wide.

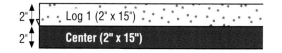

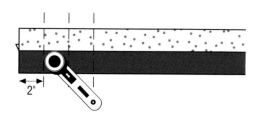

2. With Log 1 closest to you, place the quick-pieced center units on top of the Log 2 strip, positioning them as close together as possible without overlapping edges. Stitch. Cut between the squares, trimming away any excess fabric between the units. Press seams away from the center square.

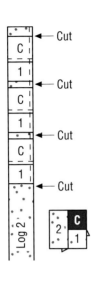

3. With Log 2 closest to you, place just-completed units on top of a Log 3 strip, positioning them as close together as possible without overlapping edges. Stitch. Cut between the units, trimming away any excess fabric between the units. Press seams away from the center square.

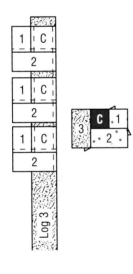

4. With Log 3 closest to you, place just-completed units on top of a Log 4 strip, positioning them as close together as possible without overlapping edges. Stitch. Cut between the units and press as described above.

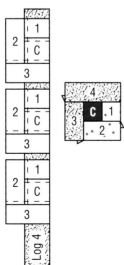

5. Continue adding logs in numerical order as described above to complete 6 Log Cabin blocks.

> ### Tip
> When sewing units to log strips, always place the last strip you added closest to you. Always press seams away from the center square.

6. Arrange the blocks as shown below. Sew blocks together in horizontal rows; press seams in opposite directions from row to row.
7. Sew rows together, making sure to match the seams between the blocks.

Quilt Finishing

1. Sew the inner border strips to the sides first, then to the top and bottom edges of the quilt top. Repeat with the outer border strips. See page 10.
2. Layer the quilt top with batting and backing; baste. Quilt as desired.
3. Bind the edges of the quilt. See pages 13–15.

Log Cabin Zoo

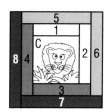

Make 6.

Color Photo: Animal Crackers on page 21
Quilt Size: 38½" x 50½"
Finished Block Size: 12"

Materials *44"-wide fabric*		Cutting *Cut all strips across the fabric width.*		
		First Cut		**Second Cut**
	Yardage	*No. of Strips*	*Strip Size*	*Dimensions*
Center squares	¼ yd.*	1	6½" x 42"	6 ☐ – 6½" x 6½"
Light 1	¼ yd.	3	2" x 42" for Logs 1 and 2	
Light 2	⅜ yd.	4	2" x 42" for Logs 5 and 6	
Dark 1	¼ yd.	3	2" x 42" for Logs 3 and 4	
Dark 2	⅜ yd.	4	2" x 42" for Logs 7 and 8	
Inner border (sides)	¼ yd.	2	1" x 36½"	
(top/bottom)		2	1" x 25½"	
Outer border (sides)	1 yd.	2	7" x 37½"	
(top/bottom)		2	7" x 38½"	
Binding	½ yd.	5	2½" x 42"	
Backing	1⅝ yds.			

*You will need additional yardage if you want to center specific design motifs within each square.

Quilt Top Assembly

1. Place the squares on top of Log 1, right sides together**. Position them as close together as possible without overlapping edges. Stitch. Cut between the squares, trimming away any excess fabric between the units. Press the seams away from the center square.

   ** If you cut the squares with an animal motif in the center of each, begin with the top of the center square to the right so the first strip you add is at the top of the block.

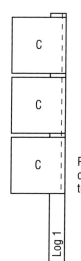

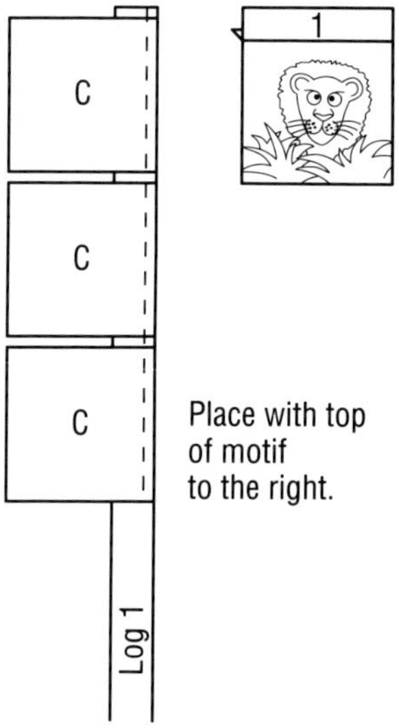

Place with top of motif to the right.

2. With Log 1 closest to you, place the center units on top of a strip for Log 2. Position them as close together as possible without overlapping edges. Stitch. Cut between the units, trimming away any excess fabric between the units. Press the seams away from the center square.

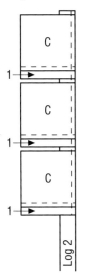

3. With Log 2 closest to you, place just-completed units on top of a strip for Log 3. Position them as close together as possible without overlapping edges. Stitch. Cut and press as described above.

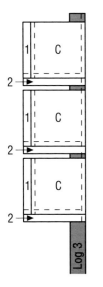
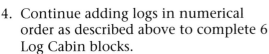

4. Continue adding logs in numerical order as described above to complete 6 Log Cabin blocks.

Tip

When sewing units to log strips, always place the last strip you added closest to you. Always press seams away from the center square.

5. Arrange blocks as shown below. Sew blocks together in horizontal rows; press seams in opposite directions from row to row.
6. Sew the rows together, making sure to match the seams between each block.

Quilt Finishing

1. Sew the inner border to the sides first, then to the top and bottom edges of the quilt top. Repeat with the outer border strips. See page 10.
2. Layer the quilt top with batting and backing; baste. Quilt as desired.
3. Bind the edges of the quilt. See pages 13–15.

Courthouse Steps

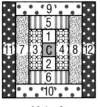

Make 9.

Color Photo: Jelly Bean Jungle on page 22
Quilt Size: 42" x 42"
Finished Block Size: 10½"

	Materials *44"-wide fabric*		Cutting *Cut all strips across the fabric width.*	
	Yardage	**No. of Strips**	**Strip Size**	
Center	⅛ yd.	1	2" x 42"	
Light 1	¼ yd.	2	2" x 42" for Logs 1 and 2	
Light 2	¼ yd.	3	2" x 42" for Logs 5 and 6	
Light 3	⅜ yd.	4	2" x 42" for Logs 9 and 10	
Dark 1	¼ yd.	3	2" x 42" for Logs 3 and 4	
Dark 2	⅜ yd.	4	2" x 42" for Logs 7 and 8	
Dark 3	½ yd.	6	2" x 42" for Logs 11 and 12	
Inner border (sides)	¼ yd.	2	1½" x 32"	
(top/bottom)		2	1½" x 34"	
Outer border (sides)	⅝ yd.	2	4½" x 34"	
(top/bottom)		2	4½" x 42"	
Binding	½ yd.	5	2½" x 42"	
Backing	2⅝ yds.*			

*See page 11 for backing options.

Quilt Top Assembly

1. To quick piece the three squares in the center of the block, sew 1 strip set as shown at right. Crosscut the strip set into 9 segments, each 2" wide for the center units. Press seams away from center strip.

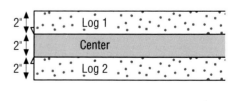

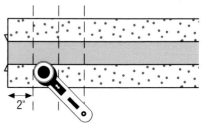

2. Place center units on top of a strip for Log 3. Position as close together as possible without overlapping edges. Stitch. Cut between the squares, trimming away any excess fabric between the units. Press the seams away from the center square.

3. Place just-completed units on top of a strip for Log 4. Position as close together as possible without overlapping edges. Stitch. Cut between the units, trimming away excess fabric between the units. Press the seams away from the center square.

4. Place units on top of a strip for Log 5. Position, stitch, trim, and press as described above.

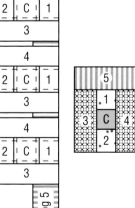

5. Continue adding logs in numerical order as described above to complete 9 Courthouse Steps blocks.
6. Arrange the blocks as shown. Sew the blocks together in horizontal rows. Press the seams in opposite directions from row to row.
7. Sew the rows together, making sure to match the seams between the blocks.

Quilt Finishing

1. Sew the inner border to the sides first, then to the top and bottom edges of the quilt top. Repeat with the outer border strips. See page 10.
2. Layer the quilt top with batting and backing; baste. Quilt as desired.
3. Bind the edges of the quilt. See pages 13–15.

Hourglass

Make 12.

Color Photo: Confetti Sparkler on page 23
Quilt Size: 38¼" x 46½"
Finished Block Size: 8¼"

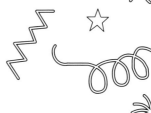

Materials
44"-wide fabric

Cutting
Cut all strips across the fabric width.

	Yardage	First Cut		Second Cut
		No. of Strips	Strip Size	Dimensions
5 Hourglass fabrics	⅛ yd. each	2 from each fabric	1¾" x 42"	
Background	⅝ yd.	2	9½" x 42"	6 ◨ – 9½" x 9½"*
Inner border (sides)	⅜ yd.	2	2½" x 33½"	
(top/bottom)		2	2½" x 29¼"	
Outer border (sides)	¾ yd.	2	5" x 37½"	
(top/bottom)		2	5" x 38¼"	
Binding	½ yd.	5	2½" x 42"	
Backing	1½ yds.			

*See step 4 in "Quilt Top Assembly" for additional cutting directions.

Quilt Top Assembly

1. Make 2 strip sets as shown at right, varying the placement of the 5 Hourglass fabrics in each strip set. Press seams in the same direction.

Make 2 strip sets, with fabrics arranged in different order for each set.

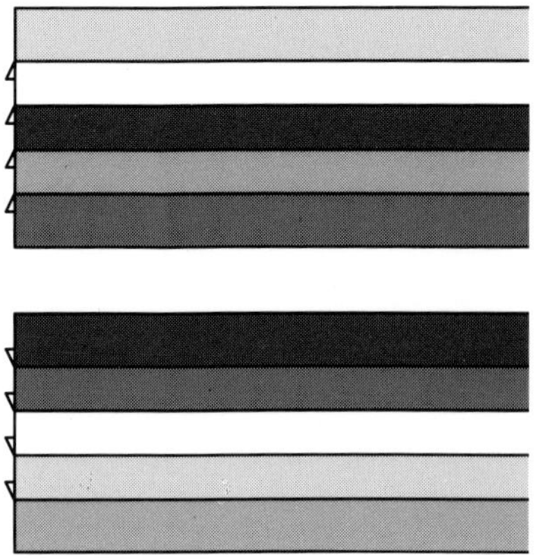

2. Crosscut the strip sets into 12 squares, each 6¾" x 6¾"*****.

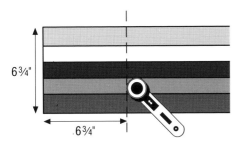

6¾"

6¾"

**Measure the width of the strip sets. If they are not 6¾" wide, then crosscut the strip sets into squares, using the width of the strip set for the size. For example, if your strip set is only 6¹/₄" wide, crosscut the strip set into 6¹/₄" squares. The end result must be a square block.*

3. Cut the 12 squares once diagonally to yield 24 half-square triangles.

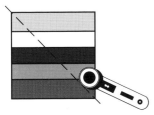

4. Stack the 9½" background squares in sets of three. Cut each stack twice diagonally for 24 quarter-square triangles.

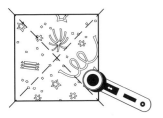 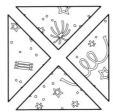

5. Make 12 Hourglass blocks as shown, using the pieced half-square triangles and the quarter-square triangles cut from background fabric.

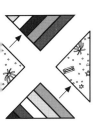 

6. Arrange the blocks as shown below. Sew the blocks together in horizontal rows and press the seams in opposite directions from row to row.
7. Sew the rows together, making sure to match the seams between the blocks.

Quilt Finishing

1. Sew the inner border strips to the sides first, then to the top and bottom edges of the quilt top. Repeat with the outer border strips. See page 10.
2. Layer the quilt top with batting and backing; baste. Quilt as desired.
3. Bind the edges of the quilt. See pages 13–15.

Friendship Star

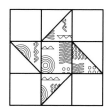

Make 6.

Color Photo: A Star is Born! on page 24
Quilt Size: 36½" x 47½"
Finished Block Size: 9"

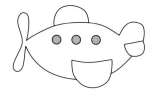

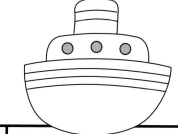

Materials *44"-wide fabric*		Cutting *Cut all strips across the fabric width.*		
	Yardage	**First Cut**		**Second Cut**
		No. of Strips	Strip Size	Dimensions
Stars	⅜ yd.*	2	3⅞" x 42"	12 ▦ – 3⅞" x 3⅞"
		1	3½" x 42"	6 ▦ – 3½" x 3½"
Background	½ yd.	2	3⅞" x 42"	12 ▦ – 3⅞" x 3⅞"
		2	3½" x 42"	24 ▦ – 3½" x 3½"
Sashing	¼ yd.	2	2½" x 42"**	
Inner border (sides)	⅜ yd.	2	2½" x 31½"	
(top/bottom)		2	2½" x 24½"	
Outer border (sides)	⅞ yd.	2	6½" x 35½"	
(top/bottom)		2	6½" x 36½"	
Binding	½ yd.	5	2½" x 42"	
Backing	1½ yds.			

*This yardage is for making all the stars from the same print. To make each star from a different print, purchase ⅛ yd. of 6 different prints. Cut 2 squares, each 3⅞" x 3⅞", and 1 square, 3½" x 3½", from each print.

**See step 3 in "Quilt Top Assembly" for additional cutting directions.

Quilt Top Assembly

1. Make 24 half-square triangle units as shown on pages 8–9, using the 3⅞" squares cut from the star and background fabrics.

Make 24.

2. Make 6 Star blocks as shown.

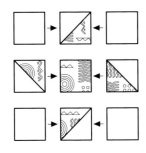

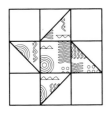

3. From the strips for the sashing, cut:
   2 strips, each 2½" x 20½", for the horizontal sashing strips between the rows of blocks
   3 strips, each 2½" x 9½", for the vertical sashing strips between the blocks.

4. Arrange the blocks and sashing strips as shown. Sew blocks together in horizontal rows, adding the 9½" sashing strips between the blocks. Sew rows together, adding the 20½" sashing strips between the rows.

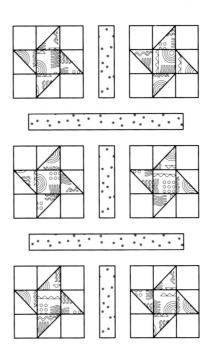

Quilt Finishing

1. Sew the inner border to the sides first, then to the top and bottom edges of the quilt top. Repeat with the strips for the outer border. See page 10.
2. Layer the quilt top with batting and backing; baste. Quilt as desired.
3. Bind the edges of the quilt. See pages 13–15.

Shoo Fly

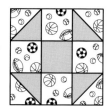

Make 6.

Color Photo: Sports Rally on page 27
Quilt Size: 38½" x 51"
Finished Block Size: 10½"

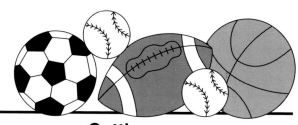

Materials 44"-wide fabric		Cutting Cut all strips across the fabric width.		
		First Cut		**Second Cut**
	Yardage	*No. of Strips*	*Strip Size*	*Dimensions*
Fabric A	½ yd.	2	4⅜" x 42"	12 ▢ – 4⅜" x 4⅜"
		1	4" x 42"	6 ▢ – 4" x 4"
Fabric B	¾ yd.	2	4⅜" x 42"	12 ▢ – 4⅜" x 4⅜"
		3	4" x 42"	24 ▢ – 4" x 4"
Sashing	½ yd.	6	2½" x 42"	17 ▭ – 2½" x 11"
Cornerstones	⅛ yd.	1	2½" x 42"	12 ▢ – 2½" x 2½"
Inner border (sides)	¼ yd.	2	1½" x 40"	
(top/bottom)		2	1½" x 29½"	
Outer border (sides)	¾ yd.	2	5" x 42"	
(top/bottom)		2	5" x 38½"	
Binding	½ yd.	5	2½" x 42"	
Backing	1⅝ yds.			

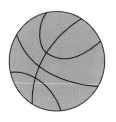

Quilt Top Assembly

1. Make 24 half-square triangle units as shown on pages 8–9, using the 4⅜" squares cut from Fabric A and Fabric B.

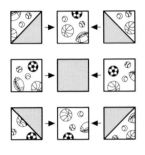

Make 24.

2. Make 6 Shoo Fly blocks as shown below.

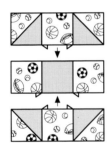

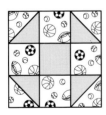

3. Arrange blocks, sashing strips, and cornerstones as shown below.

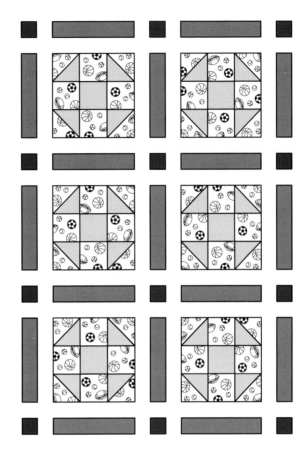

4. Sew cornerstones and sashing strips together in horizontal rows. Press the seams toward the sashing strips.
5. Sew the sashing strips and blocks together in horizontal rows. Press the seams toward the sashing strips.
6. Sew the rows together, making sure to match the seams between the blocks.

Quilt Finishing

1. Sew the inner border strips to the sides first, then to the top and bottom edges of the quilt top. Repeat with the outer border strips. See page 10.
2. Layer the quilt top with batting and backing; baste. Quilt as desired.
3. Bind the edges of the quilt. See pages 13–15.

Easy Attic Windows

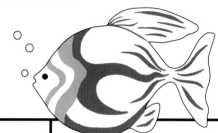

Color Photos: Mickey in the Attic on page 27
and Something's Fishy in the Attic on page 26
Quilt Size: 38½" x 38½"
Finished Block Size: 8"

Make 9.

Materials 44"-wide fabric		Cutting Cut all strips across the fabric width.		
		First Cut		Second Cut
	Yardage	No. of Strips	Strip Size	Dimensions
Feature Fabric	½ yd.*	2	6½" x 42"	9 — 6½" x 6½"
Light Window	⅜ yd.	2	2½" x 42"	9 — 2½" x 6½"
		1	2⅞" x 42"	5 — 2⅞" x 2⅞"
Dark Window	⅜ yd.	2	2½" x 42"	9 — 2½" x 6½"
		1	2⅞" x 42"	5 — 2⅞" x 2⅞"
Sashing	¼ yd.	3	1½" x 42"**	
Inner border (sides)	¼ yd.	2	1½" x 26½"	
(top/bottom)		2	1½" x 28½"	
Outer border (sides)	¾ yd.	2	5½" x 28½"	
(top/bottom)		2	5½" x 38½"	
Binding	⅜ yd.	4	2½" x 42"	
Backing	1¼ yds.			

*You will need additional yardage if you want to center specific design motifs within each square.
**See step 3 in "Quilt Top Assembly" for additional cutting directions.

Quilt Top Assembly

1. Make 9 half-square triangle units as shown on pages 8–9, using the 2⅞" squares cut from the light and dark window fabrics.

Make 9.

2. Make 9 Attic Window blocks as shown below.

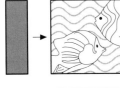

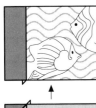

3. From the strips for the sashing, cut:
   2 pieces, each 1½" x 26½", for the horizontal sashing between the rows
   6 pieces, each 1½" x 8½", for the vertical sashing strips between blocks.

4. Arrange the blocks and the sashing strips as shown below. Sew the blocks and the vertical sashing strips together in horizontal rows.

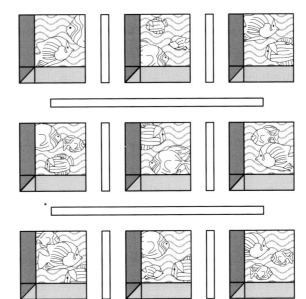

5. Sew the rows together, adding the long sashing strips between the rows.

Quilt Finishing

1. Sew the inner border strips to the sides first, then to the top and bottom edges of the quilt top. Repeat with the outer border strips. See page 10.
2. Layer the quilt top with batting and backing; baste. Quilt as desired.
3. Bind the edges of the quilt. See pages 13–15.

You might also enjoy these other fine titles from

Martingale & Company

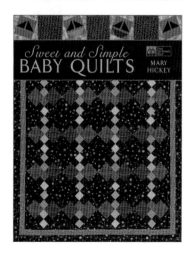

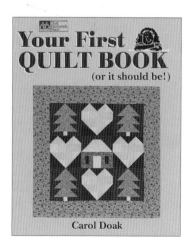

Our books are available at bookstores and your favorite craft, fabric, and yarn retailers.

Visit us at www.martingale-pub.com or contact us at:

That Patchwork Place®

America's Best-Loved Quilt Books®

Martingale®
& C O M P A N Y

America's Best-Loved Craft & Hobby Books®
America's Best-Loved Knitting Books®

1-800-426-3126

International: 1-425-483-3313
Fax: 1-425-486-7596
Email: info@martingale-pub.com